THIS BOOK BELONGS TO:

CONTACT INFORMATION	
NAME:	
ADDRESS:	
PHONE:	

START / END DATES

_____ / / _____   TO   _____ / / _____

Dedication

This Quinceanera Guest Book is dedicated to all the birthday girls out there who are turning 15 and want to remember their guests and document their findings in the process.

You are my inspiration for producing books and I'm honored to be a part of keeping all of your Quinceanera Guest Book notes and records organized.

This journal notebook will help you record the details of your guests.

Thoughtfully put together with these sections to record: Contact Info, Name, Date, Location, Family Tree, Guests, Thoughts & Wishes From Guests, Gift Log, & Special Memories.

How to Use this Book

The purpose of this book is to keep all of your Quinceanera guest notes all in one place. It will help keep you organized.

This Quinceanera Guest Book will allow you to accurately document details about your guests.

Here are examples of the prompts for you to fill in and write about your experience in this book:

1. Contact Information - Write your contact info.

2. Name Of Quinceanera - Record the name of the birthday girl.

3. Date, Location - Log the date & location.

4. Parents, Grandparents, And Siblings Names - Fill out your family tree information.

5. Name Of Guest/ Guests - Guests can write their names.

6. Thoughts And Wishes - Guests can write their thoughts and wishes.

7. Gift Log - Record gifts received.

In Celebration of

_____

Date

_____

Location

_____

parents

_____

_____

grand parents

_____

_____

_____

_____

_____

siblings

_____

_____

_____

_____

_____

gift log

GIFT DESCRIPTION	GIVEN BY	THANK YOU NOTE SENT	
		YES	NO
		YES	NO
		YES	NO
		YES	NO
		YES	NO
		YES	NO
		YES	NO
		YES	NO
		YES	NO
		YES	NO
		YES	NO
		YES	NO
		YES	NO
		YES	NO
		YES	NO
		YES	NO

gift log

GIFT DESCRIPTION	GIVEN BY	THANK YOU NOTE SENT	
		YES	NO
		YES	NO
		YES	NO
		YES	NO
		YES	NO
		YES	NO
		YES	NO
		YES	NO
		YES	NO
		YES	NO
		YES	NO
		YES	NO
		YES	NO
		YES	NO
		YES	NO
		YES	NO

guest book

name

thoughts & wishes

special memories

guest book

name

thoughts & wishes

special memories

guest book

name

thoughts & wishes

special memories

guest book

name

thoughts & wishes

special memories

guest book

name

thoughts & wishes

special memories

guest book

name

thoughts & wishes

special memories

guest book

name

thoughts & wishes

special memories

guest book

name

thoughts & wishes

special memories

guest book

name

thoughts & wishes

special memories

guest book

name

thoughts & wishes

special memories

guest book

name

thoughts & wishes

special memories

guest book

name

thoughts & wishes

special memories

guest book

name

thoughts & wishes

special memories

guest book

name   thoughts & wishes

special memories

guest book

name

thoughts & wishes

special memories

guest book

name

thoughts & wishes

special memories

guest book

name

thoughts & wishes

special memories

guest book

name

thoughts & wishes

special memories

guest book

name

thoughts & wishes

special memories

guest book

name

thoughts & wishes

special memories

guest book

name

thoughts & wishes

special memories

guest book

name

thoughts & wishes

special memories

guest book

name

thoughts & wishes

special memories

guest book

name   thoughts & wishes

special memories

guest book

name

thoughts & wishes

special memories

guest book

name

thoughts & wishes

special memories

guest book

name

thoughts & wishes

special memories

guest book

name

thoughts & wishes

special memories

guest book

name

thoughts & wishes

special memories

guest book

name

thoughts & wishes

special memories

guest book

name

thoughts & wishes

special memories

guest book

name

thoughts & wishes

special memories

guest book

name

thoughts & wishes

special memories

guest book

name

thoughts & wishes

special memories

guest book

name

thoughts & wishes

special memories

guest book

name

thoughts & wishes

special memories

guest book

name

thoughts & wishes

special memories

guest book

name

thoughts & wishes

special memories

guest book

name

thoughts & wishes

special memories

guest book

name

thoughts & wishes

special memories

guest book

name

thoughts & wishes

special memories

guest book

name

thoughts & wishes

special memories

guest book

name

thoughts & wishes

special memories

guest book

name

thoughts & wishes

special memories

guest book

name

thoughts & wishes

special memories

guest book

name

thoughts & wishes

special memories

www.ingramcontent.com/pod-product-compliance
Lightning Source LLC
Chambersburg PA
CBHW080601030426

42336CB00019B/3282